MEM⚙RY
MECHANICS

MEM⚙RY MECHANICS

How to Memorize Anything

Gary DeMar

American Vision Press

Powder Springs, Georgia

American Vision

A Biblical Worldview Ministry

American Vision, Inc.
3150 Florence Road, Suite 2
Powder Springs, Georgia 30127-5385
www.AmericanVision.org
1-800-628-9460

Layout design by Luis Lovelace
Cover by Joseph Darnell
Illustrations by Adam Stiles

ISBN-13: 978-0-915815-89-0

Dedicated to

Dr. D. James Kennedy

(1930–2007)

who introduced me to the
marvels of memory mechanics

Contents

1

How I Developed a Duct-Tape Memory

The light was blinking on the answering machine. It was a message telling my wife that her new glasses were ready. When she came in to pick them up, she was to give her name and tell the salesperson that the glasses would be in "Drawer 1195." Immediately, I blurted out "toad pill." My wife is used to me making odd associations to things that have just been said. It's the way my quirky mind works. In a very calm but bracing voice, a little afraid of what she was about to hear, she asked me what a "toad pill" was. I told her it was a way to remember 1195. "Toad," I told her, "represented the number 11, while "pill" represented the number 95. To remember the number, I would visualize a toad swallowing a giant pill as he hopped to a drawer wearing large glasses."

This is just one memory technique that I'll share with you in this innovative book. The innovation is not in the

> *"Memory… is the diary that we all carry about with us."*
> —Oscar Wilde

techniques but in their presentation. Most memory books include many of the techniques that are presented in *Memory Mechanics*. Some even include a few illustrations. *Memory Mechanics* not only describes the techniques but applies them with vivid and memorable visuals. It practices what it claims to teach. In the end you will learn why "toad pill" is 1195 and why it can help you develop a Duct-Tape memory so what you memorize will "stick" in your mind.

I was not a very good student. Some of this can be attributed to the fact that I was not interested in what was being taught. So instead of studying, I spent a considerable amount of time pursuing an athletic career. At the end of my junior year in high school, I started to receive letters from colleges interested in my athletic ability. I was ranked as one of the top five shot putters in the nation. Here was the problem. My grades were so bad that I did not meet the academic qualifying standards set by the National Collegiate Athletic Association (NCAA). I had more than 40 scholarship offers to some of the most prestigious colleges in the nation, but I could not use any of them. I ended up attending a non-NCAA school for one semester hoping to improve my grades enough so I could take advantage of the scholarship offers. I eventually transferred and graduated from Western Michigan University in 1973. The first two years of college were a challenge, juggling academics with my athletic scholarship obligations. But I did it. Along the way, I began to study and apply some memory techniques I had learned. They changed my life!

> *"The sense of sight is the strongest of all the senses."*
> —Frances A. Yates

When I was 24, I decided to go on to graduate school, attending Reformed Theological Seminary in Jackson, Mississippi. Before being accepted, I needed a year of Greek and a year of Bible. These two pre-seminary courses were taught during a ten-week period during the summer of 1974, two hours each day for each class. I went to bed at 10:00 each evening and got up at 4:00 in the morning. I showered, ate breakfast, and studied until 7:30. Then I was off to two hours of Greek, followed by a 30 minute break, and then two hours of Bible. By 12:45 I was back home, eating lunch and hitting the books again until dinner and then to bed at 10:00. I didn't deviate from this schedule for ten weeks.

The seminary curriculum was rigorous, including three years of advanced Greek and Hebrew, Aramaic, as an elective, philosophy, apologetics, history, and ecclesiology. The few memory techniques I had picked up while in college were not enough to get me through these courses. Just prior to leaving for seminary, Dr. D. James Kennedy introduced me to a memory course developed by David Roth. Applying his techniques to Greek and Hebrew was a lifesaver. They really came in handy when I had to learn long lists of terms and events. In a New Testament course, we had to learn the events in the life of Christ in order. There were nearly 100 of them. I learned them in less than 30 minutes. I'll show you the technique I used.

Since graduating from college and seminary and earning a Ph.D., I have written more than 25 books. My memory isn't any better than it was in high school, but by applying the techniques outlined in this book, I give the appearance to a lot of people that I'm a whole lot smarter than I really am. After learning and applying these principles, you can fool them too.

2

"I forgot!"

You have said it thousands of times with embarrassment, vexation, and self-reproach. In attempting to remember speeches, price lists, studies, statistics, names, and faces you have depended on the old, tiresome method of repetition to stamp them on your memory—and it went back on you at the critical moment.

This is all unnecessary. You have the proper mental equipment, but neglect and wrong methods have caused it to deteriorate.

Your memory is actually the most wonderful instrument in the world. You need only to know how to use it to do things that appear marvelous. The purpose of these lessons is to afford you a real opportunity for improvement.[1]

The brain is a magnificent creation. A typical adult's brain contains fifteen billion to one hundred billion neurons. If we accept the lower estimate, this means that you and I can remember two-to-the-ten-billionth-power bits of information. How big is this number? It would

> "Of all the faculties of the human mind that of memory is the first which suffers decay from age."
> —*Thomas Jefferson*

take you ninety years to write out the number if you wrote a zero per second. If we take the larger number of neurons, this would be equivalent to ten billion encyclopedia pages of information. The brain is a big place in a very small space.[2]

Some see the brain as a highly evolved machine. It's not. There is something unique about the human brain and its relationship with the mind. The mind picks, evaluates, sorts, compares, discards, and formulates stored information in less than a split second. An evaluation process goes on in the mind that dumb atoms could not produce and no computer can match.

> The key word here is *evaluating*. By placing a value on a bit of information we let it advance to the forefront or recede to form a part of a larger picture. We can do this temporarily or permanently, and we can convert the images later if we want to. No tape recorder, camera, or even a computer can do all of this. Computers, in fact, are just very fast, efficient morons, with neither imagination nor common sense.[3]

As scientists learn more about memory, they are beginning to realize that there is no single entity called "memory." Consider an amnesiac. Clive Wearing once was an expert on Renaissance music and a producer for the British Broadcasting Corporation (BBC). Not long ago he came down with a rare form of encephalitis, an inflammation of the brain, which left him with a memory span of only a few seconds. He cannot recall a single event in the past. He couldn't tell you what he just had for lunch, even if he had eaten the meal ten minutes before. But not all his memory patterns have been wiped out. He can sing and conduct a choir. His musical ability is still intact. Wearing's wife, Deborah, says he "is trapped forever in the groove of a scratched record."[4]

A similar condition is used as the background story in the movie *50 First Dates* (2004) starring Adam Sandler and Drew Barrymore. Barrymore's character has short-term memory loss that was the result of a head injury she received in an auto accident. While her basic day-to-day memory is intact, she

> "I've a grand memory for forgetting."
> —*Robert Louis Stevenson*

can only remember new events that happen to her in a single day. When she awakens in the morning, she can't remember anything that happened the previous day. Memory is multi-faceted and much more difficult to describe and define than was once thought. "It seems, then, that some sections of the mind's archives store facts (names, images, events), while others store procedures (recollections of how to do things)."[5]

While it's important to understand what memory is, it's more important to understand how memory works and how to benefit from its built-in system designed for memorization. We all want a better memory, and there are methods that have been proven to work for everyone.

Memory Techniques

We all have an innate ability to memorize. And while superior intelligence might be an asset in developing a great memory, it's not a prerequisite. For most of us, memory is more a learned technique than a gift. The many things we know well, we've spent a lot of time doing over and over again. Repetition is the best way to develop a sticky memory. Unfortunately, repeating an action is not always possible. Sometimes we need to remember things for the moment.

There are times when a single event has been recorded in your mind for a lifetime and can be recalled in striking detail in a split second. On November 22, 1963, President John F. Kennedy was assassinated in Dallas, Texas. I can remember where

> *"Everyone has a photographic memory. Some just don't have film."*
> —Steven Wright

I was and what I was doing. Many others can recall the same experience as well as where they were and what they were doing when the Challenger exploded on January 28, 1986. The same is true of the horrible images of 9/11. If anything else of importance happened on those days, they are forever *associated* and *linked* with these vividly etched events.

As I've read more, I have been able to connect some historical facts along the way that I have linked with the events of November 22, 1963. For example, C. S. Lewis, author of *Mere Christianity* and *The Chronicles of Narnia,* also died that day as did Aldous Huxley, grandson of Thomas Huxley, "Darwin's Bulldog," and author of *Brave New World* and *The Doors of Perception,* which was the inspiration for of the musical group *The Doors.* These new *connections* have led me to more knowledge about these two men and their works. You probably have similar memory patterns. What makes these events "stick" while other events and facts slip out of our mind as if they were coated with Teflon? It's all about *links, connections, visualizations,* and *associations* we make between the familiar (what we know) and the unfamiliar (what we don't know).

The Limits of Working Memory

New studies show that some people have difficulty with something called "working memory." What is working memory? Picture a box that can only hold so many items. When a new item is added to the

full box, an item already in the box is forced out to make room for the new item. Our short-term working memory functions in a similar way. When a new item enters our memory box, it pushes out items that entered at an earlier time. The following description portrays the frustration experienced by many when they try to learn something new:

> [Dr. Mel Levine] said working memory allows a reader to remember what is at the beginning of the page when reaching the end of the page. Kids with trouble with active working memory get lost in the middle.
>
> "One little girl told me recently, 'Every time I read a sentence it erases the one that was before it,'" Levine said in a telephone interview. "That's a perfect example of an active working memory dysfunction."
>
> Memory training may help improve working memory. "The claims that are being made are that all of the attention-related aspects of processing and working memory can be trained," [Nelson] Cowan [a cognitive psychologist at the University of Missouri] said.[6]

The trick is finding ways to link the items that are pushed out of the box with the new items being put into the box so the earlier information is not lost. In effect, a chain is created to link the items that are pushed out of the memory box with those already in the box.

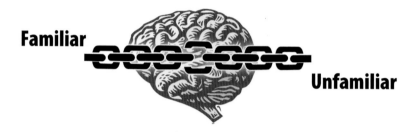

Familiar **Unfamiliar**

I can identify with those who have a dysfunctional "working memory." I've struggled with the problem all my life, especially in math. It never gets better because it's a problem that resides in the way my brain works. That's why I still have to rely on memory devices like those in this book to help me retain new information.

Long-term memory is different. Much of what we remember sticks in our mind because of repetition. That's how we learned to speak, read, and write. Learning to ride a bicycle, drive a car, play a musical instrument, or learn a sport came by way of repetition. We struggled when we first got on a bicycle, but with practice, riding became almost second nature. The more we rode, the better we got. Scientists are discovering that this type of memory goes through a chemical process called long-term potentiation (LTP) that strengthens the synapses that are important to memory retention.[7]

My library contains about 25,000 different book titles, and I can tell you something about nearly every book—where it's located on the shelves, if it's a paperback or hardback, where I got it, the color of the cover, if the cover's ripped, whether it has a sewn or glued binding, the publisher, and other details too trivial to mention. How do I know these things? Did I sit down to memorize these details? I didn't. My mind works in pictures and odd and seemingly unrelated associations. Also, I work with these books every day. It's my life's work. But if someone challenged me to memorize the titles of ten random books, it would be a supreme effort unless I applied a number of the memory techniques discussed in *Memory Mechanics.*

There isn't enough time for repetitive learning when it comes to preparing for a history or biology test. This is where short-term memory techniques are most helpful. It's a way to increase the size of your working memory box by linking with items that are pushed out when new items are dropped in without getting a brain transplant or a brain boost.

Mnemonics

The ability to memorize can improve by using proven mnemonic techniques. The word mnemonics (pronounced *ne-MON-iks*) is derived from a Greek root word that makes up the name of Mnemosyne ("remembrance"), the personification of memory in Greek mythology. Mnemosyne was the mother of the nine sister muses who presided over the arts and sciences. Our English word *mnemonic* means "helpful to memory."

The memory mechanics discussed in this book do not require a high IQ, an advanced academic degree, or even a good innate ability to remember. They are techniques that can be learned by anyone, and they work!

In fourteen hundred and ninety-two Columbus sailed the ocean blue.

Most learning comes by way of *associations*. We connect—associate—what we do know with what we are trying to learn and retain. Most learning takes place this way at a subconscious level. We look for some relationship between the

new material and the *familiar material*. While there may not be a subject connection (e.g., room and house), there may be an auditory connection ("In fourteen hundred and ninety-two Columbus sailed the ocean *blue*").

> "Memory is the library of the mind."
> —*Francis Fauvel-Gourand*

Two and *blue* have no subject connection, but they do sound alike. As we will see, there are ways to force memory connections where none initially existed.

3

Making Memory Connections

Memory techniques have a long history, for example, Psalm 119, the longest Psalm in the Bible, is made up of 176 verses in 22 groups of 8 verses. It is designed to be memorized. To make memorization easier, each of the 22 groups begins each verse in each group with a letter of the Hebrew alphabet. For example, the first letter in the first group of 8 verses begins with the letter *aleph* (verses 1–8), the first letter of the Hebrew alphabet. The next group of 8 verses begins with *beth* (9–16). This continues until the final letter *tav*. You'll need a Hebrew Bible to see the pattern. A similar memory device is used in Psalm 9, with two verses for each of the 22 Hebrew consonants (there are no vowels in the Hebrew alphabet).[8] The familiar (the Hebrew alphabet) is linked to the unfamiliar (the content of the verses). The memory technique of grouping is also employed.

In the fifteenth century, block books were created to help clergymen teach the content of the Bible through the use of visuals. Keep in mind that books of any kind were difficult to produce, expensive to print, and a luxury to own. The most widely used instructional block book was the *Biblia pauperum* (*Bible of the Poor* or *The Pauper's Bible*) that portrayed the events of the historical books of the Bible using easily identifiable symbols. Here's a modern rendition from the Gospel of Matthew (chapters 19–24)[9] based on a black and white illustration:

19. The union of husband and wife in marriage.

20. The hired laborers in the vineyard.

21. Jesus enters Jerusalem on a donkey.

22. The great wedding feast.

23. The Scribes and Pharisees who sit in the seat of Moses.

24. The destruction of the temple in A.D. 70 depicted as the sun and moon going dark and stars falling.

Just after a few minutes of study, you will be able to describe the main themes of Matthew 19 through 24 because of the visual imagery.

If I were to ask you to name the Great Lakes, you might be able to remember two or three of them. But if I associate the five Great Lakes with something you already know, like the word HOMES, and you picture or visualize homes floating on the five lakes, you will never forget them:

*H*uron, *O*ntario, *M*ichigan, *E*rie, and *S*uperior

HOMES identifies the first letter of the names of each of the five lakes, but how do you remember which name goes with which lake? Superior means to be above or greater than something. Lake Superior is larger and further north than the other four lakes, making it "superior." Michigan begins with the letter "M." There are two small finger lakes on either side of the large extended portion of the lake giving the lake the look of an "M." Huron is *half*way between Superior and Michigan and the two lakes to the east, Erie and Ontario. *Half*way, like Huron, begins with an "H." Lake Ontario is the eastern-most lake. If you take an "O" and cut it in half, you get what looks like two parentheses ( ). The closed parenthesis mark is at the far right (east) of the word Ontari( ). Once you get these four, the only one left is Erie. This is how my mind works. Something different might work for you, like **S**aul **M**ade **H**al **E**at **O**nions after swimming the five lakes.

Many children learned how to spell the word "arithmetic," their first big word, by saying, as they spelled out the word,

*A R*at *I*n *T*om's *H*ouse *M*ay *E*at *T*om's *I*ce *C*ream

Breaking a word into smaller parts (*arith*) and (*metic*) is also helpful when it comes to learning to spell long words. Many English words are made up of parts of other words, many from Greek and Latin prefixes, suffixes, and roots.

The colors of the light spectrum, **R**ed, **O**range, **Ye**llow, **G**reen, **B**lue, **I**ndigo, **V**iolet, can make up a fictitious man's name: **Roy G. Biv.**

The cranial nerves always present a problem for anatomy students. The following memory device is a standard to remember **O**lfactory, **O**ptic, **O**culomotor, **T**rochlear, **T**rigeminal, **A**bducens, **F**acial, **A**uditory, **G**lossopharyngeal, **V**agus, **S**pinal accessory, and **H**ypoglossal:

> **O**n **O**ld **O**lympus' **T**owering **T**op,
> **A** **F**riar **A**nd **G**reek
> **V**iewed **S**ome **H**ops.

Hopefully by the time a doctor finishes medical school, he no longer needs this memory crutch. Working in a field of study makes such artificial associations unnecessary. It's the short-term memory connections that students need.

Learning the tribes of Israel can prove to be difficult for some: Judah, Issachar, Manasseh, Benjamin, Reuben, Asher, Naphtali, Dan, Simeon, Ephraim, Gad, and Zebulun. If recalling the names is hard, look for a way to associate them with something *familiar* as was done with the color spectrum that can be easily remembered and visualized. You might try making up a song, visualizing them on a map of Israel and linking one tribe with another in an associative way, or memorizing them in groups of three or four. (This is why phone and Social Security numbers have dashes between the three groups of numbers. It's much easier to remember a long number if it is broken down into smaller groupings.)

Suppose that instead of following one of these devices (all good ones), you try taking the first letters of each tribal name to see if you can make something familiar with them. First you try B-R-I-M-S A-N-D J-E-G-S. While it might be helpful, in time you would have difficulty remembering it because it isn't familiar enough. You do a little more reconfiguring of the letters and come up with J-i-m B-r-a-n-d-s E-g-z.

J = Judah

I = Isaachar

M = Manasseh

B = Benjamin

R = Reuben

A = Asher

N = Naphtali

D = Dan

S = Simeon

E = Ephraim

G = Gad

Z = Zebulon

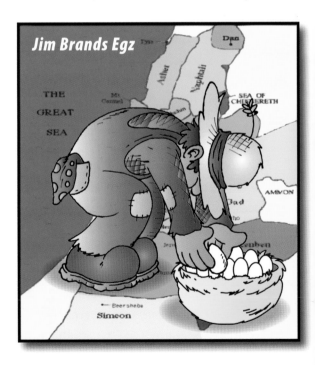

A name is easy to remember as you visualize twelve eggs with farmer Jim Brand picking them up as he stands on a map of Israel. The only variation you have to make is to change the plural for eggs (the z sound) to **egz** (the z sound substituting for the plural eggs).

It's easy to move from the tribes of Israel to the sons of Israel (Jacob). Two of the sons of Israel are not listed among the tribal allotments by name: Joseph and Levi. But there are still twelve tribes. Ephraim and Manasseh, we learn, are not the sons of Israel, but his grandsons. They are Joseph's sons, the same Joseph who is not listed among the twelve tribes. Levi is given cities throughout the tribal allotments. Ephraim and Manasseh are added to the other ten tribes and make up Joseph's inheritance.

To help you remember which kingdom is north and which is south, a division that took place after Solomon's death, try this memory trick. If you draw a large J and put a line through the middle of the letter, you can see that that this makes an **I** and a **J**. The **I** represents **I**srael (the northern kingdom), and the **J** represents **J**udah (the southern kingdom).

Acronyms

An *acronym* is a word made from the first letters of a list of names, items, places, etc. HOMES is a good example. You're probably familiar with **FACE**, an acronym used to help children remember the notes between the lines on the treble clef. SCUBA is a word

that has become a part of our vernacular: **S**elf-**C**ontained **U**nderwater **B**reathing **A**pparatus. LASER is another one: **L**ight **A**mplification by **S**timulated **E**mission of **R**adiation. This technique has its limitations since you are restricted by the first letters of the terms you are trying

to arrange in a common or uncommon word. The fact that the list may have to be in a certain order also limits the use of this technique. If an acronym just doesn't work, you'll need to go on to some other memory method.

Those taking philosophy for the first time might struggle at the beginning to keep **S**ocrates, **P**lato, and **A**ristotle in chronological order and understand the basic elements of their philosophical systems

as they are often represented in an introductory philosophy textbook. You could place the three philosophers in a **SPA** and never forget who came before whom in philosophical history: **S**ocrates, **P**lato, **A**ristotle. This technique can be expanded by applying some additional memory techniques.

Socrates is famous for his **dialogs**. He is shown holding a bowl with a log being dipped in hemlock and saying, "Can't we all just **dialog**" (dye a log)? History teaches that Socrates took the poison hemlock rather than be exiled for "corrupting the youth of Athens." The fly buzzing around Socrates' head is a reminder that Plato described his mentor as the "gadfly of Athens," who irritated the establishment similar to the way a fly irritates a horse.

Plato, a student of Socrates, is shown with his finger pointing up with an ideal **plate** (Plato) spinning in the clouds representing the eternal, ideal, unchanging Forms of things as they are manifested imperfectly in this world. The world of the senses is only an imitation of the pure, eternal, and unchanging world of the Forms. The things of this world are a poor imitation of the never-changing Forms.

Aristotle, the student of Plato, is shown gesturing to the earth, representing his belief in knowledge through observation and experience. Aristotle did not believe that ideas should be separated from the particular things we encounter in the world in which we live. Ideas are embodied in particular things that we see, touch, and experience every day. Notice that he is saying "**Air is total**-ly real. . . ," as in Aristotle.

Of course, there is much more to these philosophers and their systems, but these are some fundamental points that can get you started in learning the essentials of the great philosophers.

Acrostics

An *acrostic* is similar to an acronym. In an acronym the initials are pronounced to form a new word, either real or something pronounceable (e.g., NATO, NASA, HUD, etc.). An acrostic uses initials that are used to form words that make a memory specific sentence. For example, **E**very **G**ood **B**oy **D**oes **F**ine teaches a beginning music student the notes of the treble clef that appear on the lines: E-G-B-D-F. Students of biology have devised the following for a variety of taxonomy classifications:

Kings **P**lay **C**ards **O**n **F**airly **G**ood **S**oft **V**elvet

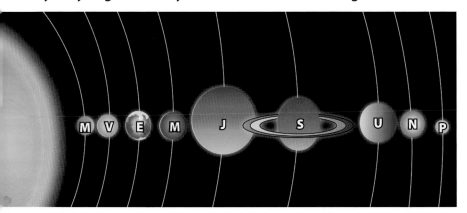

Kingdom, **P**hylum, **C**lass, **O**rder, **F**amily, **G**enus, **S**pecies, **V**ariety.

You might want to try an animal themed acrostic that begins with Domain and does not include variety (**D**omain, **K**ingdom, **P**hylum, **C**lass, **O**rder, **F**amily, **G**enus, **S**pecies):

Dumb **K**angaroos **P**lay **C**ellos, **O**rangutans **F**iddle, **G**orillas **S**ing

You can remember the planets Mercury, Venus, Earth, Mars, Jupiter, Saturn, Uranus, Neptune, and Pluto with these mnemonic devices:

My **V**ery **E**legant **M**other **J**ams **S**hells **U**nder **N**ice **P**eople

My **V**ery **E**ducated **M**other **J**ust **S**erved **U**s **N**acho **P**izza

My **V**ery **E**ager **M**emory **J**ust **S**eems **U**seful **N**aming **P**lanets

Visualization

"A picture is worth a thousand words." If that's true, then the mind can save you a lot of words. You can picture almost anything. Picture what you read. Turn abstractions into visual ideas that have a close concrete association, either in content or sound.

> *Eye-pictures are the most accurate of mental impressions.* And because the mind has this wonderful ability to see pictures long after the disappearance of the original pictures that the real eye made on the mind, we speak of the *mind's eye*, and of seeing in our *mind's eye*. The scientific name for the *mind's eye* is visualization, and the ability to use this wonderful faculty is invaluable to you.[10]

This technique can be used to study foreign languages. How many times have you associated a common English word for a foreign word 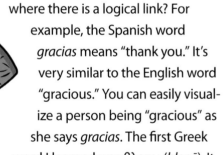 where there is a logical link? For example, the Spanish word *gracias* means "thank you." It's very similar to the English word "gracious." You can easily visualize a person being "gracious" as she says *gracias*. The first Greek word I learned was βλεπω (*blepō*). It means "I see." Our class was told to visualize a *blimp* with a big eye on it. Blimp sounds like *blepo*. The eye will remind you of "seeing." The Greek word *kosmos* (κοςμος) means "world." This is easy to remember since in English there are numerous words related to *kosmos*: cosmic, cosmology, cosmonaut, cosmopolitan, and microcosm.

What happens when the language you are studying doesn't look like or sound like English? The alphabet in Hebrew, for example, doesn't look anything like English. The 22 letters are all consonants, and you read from right to left. And unlike Latin, Greek, Spanish, and Italian there are only a few Hebrew words that are easily recognizable in English For example, the Hebrew word *shalom* is a common greeting that translates as "peace." "Amen" is derived from Hebrew and means "so be it." The English world "behemoth" is derived from a Hebrew word that means "animal" or "beast." But most Hebrew words have no English equivalent. A forced connection can be made. For example, the Hebrew word מד (pronounced *mahd*), which means "cloth," can be remembered by visualizing a woman being *mahd* when she tore the **cloth**. (For additional examples, see pages 59 and 60.) As with all long-term memory, after reading or hearing this Hebrew word numerous times, the memory association will no longer be needed.

The visualization technique can be applied to numerous areas of study. For example, the three branches of the Federal government can be visualized as a thick branch representing the Constitution with three smaller branches attached to it. Picture the image as part of a cherry tree growing in Washington, D.C. The leaves turn red and remind you of cherry **JEL**L-O for **J**udicial, **E**xecutive, and **L**egislative.

Sure, it's not always this easy, but this method will take you a long way. Visualization will come in handy when combined with other memory techniques.

The Location System

One adaptation of the visualization technique is the "Location System." According to memory researcher Daniel Schacter, using visual imagery as a memory aid in a practical way was first used by the Greek poet Simonides of Ceos (c. 556 B.C.–468 B.C.). "Simonides was the sole survivor of a roof collapse that killed all the guests at a large banquet he was attending. He was able to reconstruct the guest list by visualizing who was sitting at each seat around the table. What Simonides had discovered was that people have an astoundingly good recollection of location. In his book *Searching for Memory*, Schacter explains that this same technique was later used by Roman generals to learn the names of thousands of soldiers in their command. . . ."[11]

Roman orators commonly used the *loci* (Latin for "location") system to remember the components of a speech. They didn't have the

advantage of a Teleprompter or note cards. In this system, major parts of the speech were associated with a familiar route from the speaker's home to the Forum where he was to give his address. Along the way, he would link a familiar landmark with the points of his address. As he delivered his speech, he would recall the landmarks in order of their place along the route, and each speech component would be recalled as well.

Maybe you have a favorite route to school with some unique buildings and landmarks. One of the questions on an upcoming test is to name and discuss the most quoted thinkers used by the American founders from 1760–1805. They are, in order, of their frequency of citation: (1) Montesquieu, (2) William Blackstone, (3) John Locke, (4) David Hume, and (5) Plutarch. The first building on your route is a bank. Picture a Canadian Mountie bringing a bag of Qs to deposit in the bank. Blackstone is seen placing a black stone in the church's cemetery. John Locke tries to get gas for his car, but the pump has a big lock on it. David Hume is dressed up as the Good Humor man on his way to deliver ice cream at the hospital. Plutarch is walking his dog Pluto to get some food from the Ark Diner (Pluto + Ark = Plutarch).

If you have a group of similar concepts to learn, try placing them in a familiar environment like your home. For example, if you have to learn the names of the kings of England from Egbert of Wessex (829) to Edward Ironside (1016), you could choose several rooms with various pieces of furniture. As you walk through the house visualize, link, and associate their names with sitting in a favorite chair, playing the piano, about to jump out an open window, standing on the sofa, hanging a crown in the closet, etc. Egbert looks like an egg with a crown on his head who sits on a burnt chair by the window. Ethelwulf is your pet wolf named Ethel who is playing the piano. For king Ethelbald, picture your bald aunt Ethel looking in the mirror fixing her white wig that covers her bald head; etc. By visualizing the rooms and the furniture, you can easily recall the names by their location.

Vocalization, Rhymes, and Jingles

Some people are better auditory learners. Reading something aloud and emphasizing the main points with greater inflection may help. Most of us learned the alphabet this way as well as nursery rhymes. One way to remember names, for example, is to repeat the name of the individual you were just introduced to. Hearing it again helps the memory process. Making a familiar association with the name and its sound with some characteristic about the person also helps to cement the name with the face.

Rhyming, if you can make it work, is also a helpful memory device. I still remember a saying that was printed on my father's coffee mug that I've since learned is the essence of the "Optimist's Creed":

As you ramble on through life, Brother,
Whatever be your goal,
Keep your eye upon the doughnut,
And not upon the hole.

Here's an earlier variation:

'Twixt optimist and pessimist
The difference is droll;
The optimist the doughnut sees—
The pessimist the hole.

Henry VIII had six wives. Who was divorced, who died, and who survived? In order, from Catherine of Aragon to Kathryn Parr,

Divorced, beheaded, died,
Divorced, beheaded, survived.

Of course, you'll probably have to name each of Henry's wives. Two lists of three make the task easier:

Catherine, Anne, Jane,
Anne, Katherine, Kathryn.

Most of us can remember TV commercials because they have catchy t᷒ ᷒᷒᷒ ᷒᷒᷒᷒ ᷒᷒᷒ An old "Wheaties" jingle that first aired on

᷒ne,
᷒ine.
᷒gle (I never can keep it st᷒
᷒leys on your hands into ᷒
᷒f your pinky finger on y᷒

le bran.

31-day months, while

e corny jingle.

American poet and prodigy Winifred Sackville Stoner, Jr. came up with a handy way to remember when the Declaration of Independence was written:

> Year seventeen hundred seventy-six,
> July the fourth, this date please fix
> Within your minds, my children dear,
> for that was independence year.

One of the curiosities of history is that Thomas Jefferson and John Adams, both signatories of the Declaration, died on July 4, 1826.

In April (spring) we move our clocks ahead one hour (spring *forward*). In October (fall) we turn our clocks back one hour (fall *backward*). As a point of information, it's not Daylight *Savings* (plural) Time; it's Daylight *Saving* (singular) Time.

Here's a familiar jingle to help you remember which months have 30 days and which ones have 31:

> Thirty days hath September,
> April, June, and November;
> All the rest have thirty-one
> Excepting February alone:
> Which has twenty-eight, that's f
> 'Till leap year gives it twenty-

If you don't want to use the jing   aight), you can always turn the knuckles and   a memory device. By starting with the knuc   our left hand, begin with January. The knuc   the valleys

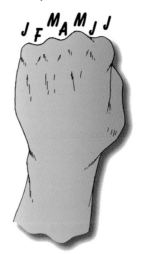 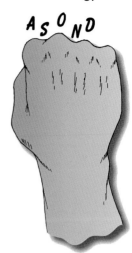

are 30-day months except, of course, February. Moving right, the valley is February. The next knuckle is March, and so on. When you get to the knuckle of your index finger, move to the knuckle on your right hand (July and August are both 31-day months) and continue until you finish with December.

Here's a jingle to help you remember the definition of the Latin phrase *quid pro quo*, literally, "something for something":

If I give something to you and get something back,
that's a *quid pro quo*, when we scratch each other's back.

Abbreviation

Sometimes it helps if you abbreviate a long section of material into its essential parts. For example:

THE TEN COMMANDMENTS

1. No other gods
2. No graven images
3. Name of Lord
4. Sabbath rest
5. Honor parents

6. No murder
7. No adultery
8. No stealing
9. No false witness
10. No coveting

Instead of Ten Commandments to learn, you now have two groups of five commandments. You can shorten this even further by leaving off the negatives. Be forewarned, however; there was a Bible published that left the "not" out of the seventh commandment. It was called the "Adulterer's Bible." The printer was heavily fined for the mistake.

There's another way to learn the Ten Commandments by using your fingers as memory prompters:

1 By holding up one finger, we are reminded there is only one God with no competitors.

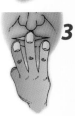

2 By holding up two fingers, we are reminded that we are not to make an image of anything to worship.

3 By holding up three fingers, covering the mouth forming a W, we are reminded to watch our "Words" about God.

4 By holding up four fingers of one hand and laying them down in the palm of your other hand, we are reminded to rest from our labors at the office (four corners of a building), our homes (four corners to a room), and our farms (four corners of a field).

5 By holding up five fingers, we are reminded of a salute, acknowledging authority, in this case the authority of our parents.

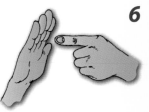

6 By holding up five fingers of one hand as a person would do in a holdup, with one finger (representing a gun) pointing to the palm of that hand, a total of six fingers, we are reminded not to murder.

7 By holding up all five fingers of one hand as a policeman would do to stop oncoming traffic, and with two fingers of the other hand behind it (representing the husband and wife), we are reminded to say no to adultery.

8 By clasping the four fingers of each hand we are reminded not to steal.

9 By holding up nine fingers (wagging with false testimony) with the tenth finger (thumb) bent (the accused), we are reminded not to bear false witness against our neighbor.

10 By holding both hands open in front of you as if grasping at everything in sight, we are reminded not to covet.

Our nation's Constitution was submitted for ratification in 1789 with an attached Bill of Rights. Here's a handy way to learn the basics of each one:

THE "BILL OF RIGHTS"

1. Freedom of **religion**, **speech**, **press**, **assembly**, **petition**

2. Right to bear **arms**

3. **Quarter**ing of soldiers

4. Search and seizure

5. Legal and Property Rights
   - Indictment
   - Double jeopardy
   - Self-incrimination
   - Legal trial
   - Private property

6. Speedy and public trial

7. Suits at common law

8. Bail, fines, punishment

9. Rights not mentioned

10. States' rights

Freedom of religion can be represented by a cross, Bible, or church building, speech by a podium, megaphone, or radio, press by a newspaper, book, or blog site, assembly by a crowd or a group of picketers holding signs, and petition by a scroll with names written on it. Arms could be represented by a rifle or a revolver. Quartering soldiers could be remembered by visualizing three soldiers coming to a home and hoping to gain entrance by paying a quarter. You can finish the visualization with your own associations.

Memory Connections

The ability to memorize a long list of items can come in handy, especially if the list needs to be in a particular order. How is this accomplished? You do it two facts at a time. By associating the first fact with the second fact, the second fact with the third fact, the third fact with the fourth fact, and so forth, you can learn a whole string of events, two facts at a time. Here's how the "Link Method" combined with the "association" and "visualization" work with learning the Minor Prophets of the Bible. First, become familiar with the list of names you need to memorize. Second, make the necessary visual connections:

1. Hosea = **Hose** spraying out **jewel**s.
2. Joel = **Jewels** falling on **a moss**-covered arrow.
3. Amos = **A moss**-covered arrow hits an **oboe-dying** musician.
4. Obadiah = The bleeding **oboe-dying** musician asks **Jonah** the "whale" for help.
5. Jonah = **Jonah** the "whale" goes to a **mic**rophone.
6. Micah = The **mic**rophone is being used by **Na**te **hum**ming.

7. Nahum = **Na**te **hum**ming wakes the **half-back**.

8. Habakkuk = The **half-back** runs into a **zeph**yr at **nigh**t.

9. Zephaniah = The **zeph**yr at **nigh**t blows over a **hag** and a **guy**.

10. Haggai = The **hag** and a **guy** scare old **Zack** and his **rye**.

11. Zechariah = **Zack** and his **rye** run to **Malachi** the mailman for help.

12. Malachi = **Malachi** the mailman delivers a complete Old Testament to be added to the books of the New Testament.

Associate each unfamiliar minor prophet with a visual sound-alike word. Visualize a *hose* (Hosea) spewing out *jewels* (Joel). The *jewels* come out and fall on a man aiming *a moss* (Amos)-covered arrow that hits a man playing an *oboe* (Obadiah), and so forth. Of course, you need to know the names of the Minor Prophets before you make the associations. The point of this exercise is to learn the 12 Minor Prophets in order.

Once you recall the hose, the visualization process takes over. The memory sequence starts with only two Minor Prophets in view at any one time. Once the memory link is made, the first Minor Prophet fades away and the new association comes into view. This technique can be used with any sequence of events or objects.

From the Abstract to the Concrete

Abstract ideas are some of the most difficult concepts to remember. An abstract idea has to be turned into something concrete. Here's a list of some abstract concepts and a list of concrete equivalents:

Abstract Concept	Concrete Symbol	Abstract Concept	Concrete Symbol
1 Intelligence		6 Hope	
2 Grief		7 Speed	
3 Peace		8 Language	
4 Ignorance		9 Happiness	
5 Security		10 Death	

Pegging and Linking

Have you ever had trouble remembering numbers, dates, or a long list of related facts or dates? Well, do I have a system for you. Most numbers and dates are abstract, but there are ways to turn them into visual representations:

   One = Foam finger

   Two = Peace sign

Four = Points of a compass

Five = Fingers on a hand

Ten = Toes on both feet

Twelve = Egg carton

Thirteen = Black cat

But this technique will only take you so far. What if you needed to memorize a list of 100 items or know the dates of 100 important historical events in order? The connection system might work for awhile, but coming up with sound-alike words and connections for 100 different items would be time consuming. Each new list would require another set of associations. There is an ingenious and better way. By learning a fixed set of 100 words, there isn't a list of items that you will not be able to memorize. I've used this system many times with fantastic results.

> "The true art of memory is the art of attention."
> —*Samuel Johnson*

4

Turning Numbers into Words

The Numeric-Phonetic method is a comprehensive memory system that uses numbers that correspond to the letter *sounds* of the alphabet. Once you memorize the ten letter sounds and their listed below, you will be able to remember a list of 100 words that are keyed to 100 numbers. Once learned, the list of number related words can be linked with the new list of items you need to memorize. With this technique, you will amaze your friends with your newly acquired ability to memorize almost anything.

Step 1: Learn the phonetic *sounds* and their numerical value.

You will need to know the basic ten letter sounds to learn and use the system. These letter sounds will be used to create a list of 100 words. Each word will match a number 1 to 100. Let's begin with a basic list of numbers and their corresponding letter *sounds*.

1	2	3	4	5	6	7	8	9	0
T	N	M	R	L	J	K	F	P	S

Notice that vowels do not have any numerical value (A E I O U), and neither do the letters W-H-Y-X. Keep in mind that it's the consonant *sounds* that are converted into numbers. The following chart expands on the other consonants and combination letters and their corresponding sounds and numerical values:

Number	Letter Sound	Memory Device
1	t, d	t and d have one downstroke and sound alike.
2	n, kn, gn	n has two downstrokes, also kn and gn since the letter combinations have the n sound.
3	m	m has three downstrokes.
4	r	R is the last letter of fouR.
5	l	L is the Roman Numeral for 50
6	j, ch, sh soft g	Backwards J looks like a 6, ch/sh and soft g and dg which only has the g sound as in "judge."
7	k, ck, hard g, c	K is made from a backward leaning 7.
8	f, ph, v	An F, joined with another turned upside down, looks like an 8. Also, V as in V8 juice.
9	p, b	Backwards p and a rotated b look like a 9 and sound alike.
0	z, s, soft c	Z as in Zero, and soft c as in cent.

Other letters that *sound like* the above letters represent the same numerical value. For example, a word with a hard "c" sound (car) and hard "g" sound (gun) would be a *7* along with *k*. A *v* could substitute for an *f* (hive). While half has an "l" in it, only the "f" sound is pronounced. This really is not very complicated, but it does take a little time to learn. **H** only has value when it is combined with other letters such as **sh**, **ch**, and **ph** since the combined letters make a single phonetic sound. Once you get these basics, the method will prove to be invaluable and a lot of fun as you find innovative ways to apply the techniques. The key is to learn the ten basic numbers and their equivalent letter sounds and then add the additional material as you go along.

Step 2: Learn the first ten words and their numerical values.

Now it's time to convert the numerical values of the letter sounds to create concrete word pictures that can be visualized and linked. Once again, keep in mind that the vowels A E I O U and the letters W-H-Y-X have no numerical value. You will notice that **Knee** is being used for 2 because the combined letters "kn" have the "n" sound. The same is true for "gn" as in "reign" or "gnome":

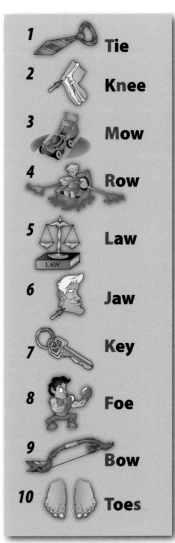

These ten words always refer to the first ten numbers. They never change.

Step 3: Link the words so you can remember them in order.

The first word, **T**ie (1), is visually and logically linked with the second word **Kn**ee (2). You might visualize a tie wrapped around a knee. A **KN**ee is then pictured pushing a man to get him to **M**ow (3) the lawn. The man who will **M**ow the lawn finds a boat to **R**ow (4) to get a set of **L**aw (5) books with scales of justice sitting on them. The Law books fall on a judge's **J**aw (6) and out falls a **K**ey (7) that's used to lock up a **F**oe (8) who wants a **B**ow (9) to shoot off someone's **T**oes (10).

You will want to make up some "sticky" associations as you *picture* the words and connect them one-by-one in your mind. Continue until you learn all ten this way. There are a total of 100 words to learn, but they all follow the same letter sound patterns with their corresponding number values (see pages 50–54). They can be learned in a few hours if you follow the linking-picturing method.

You want to be able to identify the word with the number. When you hear the number 7, you immediately know it's the word "key" because the k sound is always seven and, to repeat, the vowels A E I O U and the letters W-H-Y-X do not have any numerical value.

Here's an example of how this part of the system can work with learning a list. Let's suppose you need to learn the first ten presidents of the United States in order:

Tie = George Washington

Knee = John Adams

Mow = Thomas Jefferson

Row = James Madison

Law = James Monroe

Jaw = John Quincy Adams

Key = Andrew Jackson

Foe = Martin Van Buren

Bow = William Henry Harrison

Toes = John Tyler

1. Picture George Washington wearing a bright colored neck **tie** with a cherry tree and ax on it.
2. Picture John Adams with a **knee** to his Adam's apple.

3. Picture Thomas Jefferson about to **mow** the Declaration of Independence.

4. Picture James Madison being mad at his son because he can't **row** a boat.

5. Picture James Monroe trying to find a **law** to exhume the body of Mrs. Monroe.

6. Picture John Quincy Adams with a protruding **jaw** after he hurts his Adam's apple.

7. Picture Andrew Jackson using a **key** to get the jack out of his son's car.

8. Picture Martin Van Buren being the **foe** of the moving van company because it dropped his bureau.

9. Picture William Henry Harrison picking up a **bow** to shoot his hairy son.

10. Picture John Tyler with ten **toes** tied together tightly.

Notice how I added other memory techniques in each of the above examples to help with memorization.

Since you know the ten linking words, it's just a matter of recalling one word at a time until you get all ten. Theoretically, you could learn a list of 100 items in order in less than 30 minutes and recall the chronological list the next day for a test.

Step 4: Learn the list of 100 words and their numerical values.

Once you have mastered the first ten picture words and their corresponding letter sounds, you are on your way to learning the other 90. While the first ten words only require a single phonetic sound, the next 89 will require two, with 100 being the only number to require three (Daises). Follow the same procedure you used for the first ten words making sure you link each word with the next one.

1 Tie
2 Knee
3 Mow
4 Row
5 Law
6 Jaw
7 Key
8 Foe
9 Bow
10 Toes
11 Toad
12 Ton
13 Dam
14 Door
15 Doll
16 Dish
17 Dog
18 Dove
19 Tub
20 Nose

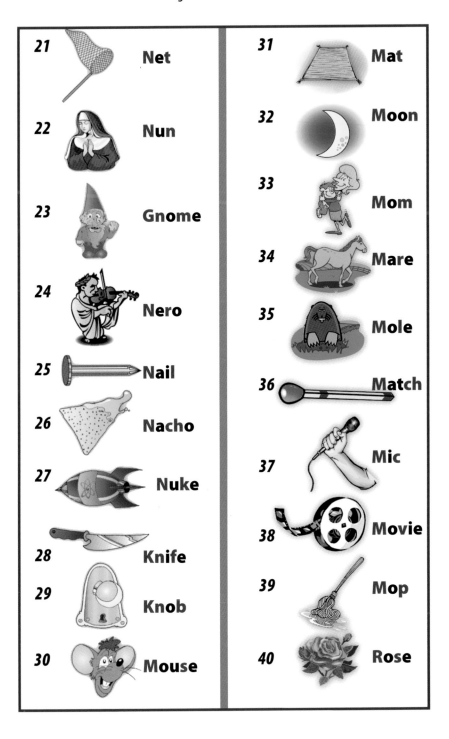

21	Net	31	Mat
22	Nun	32	Moon
23	Gnome	33	Mom
24	Nero	34	Mare
25	Nail	35	Mole
26	Nacho	36	Match
27	Nuke	37	Mic
28	Knife	38	Movie
29	Knob	39	Mop
30	Mouse	40	Rose

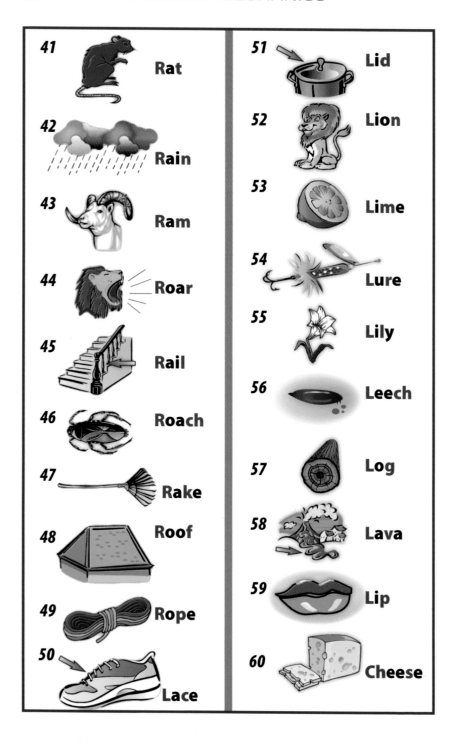

41 Rat

42 Rain

43 Ram

44 Roar

45 Rail

46 Roach

47 Rake

48 Roof

49 Rope

50 Lace

51 Lid

52 Lion

53 Lime

54 Lure

55 Lily

56 Leech

57 Log

58 Lava

59 Lip

60 Cheese

61	Jet	71	Cat
62	Chain	72	Coin
63	Chime	73	Gum
64	Chair	74	Car
65	Jail	75	Coal
66	Judge	76	Cage
67	Jug	77	Cake
68	Chef	78	Cave
69	Ship	79	Cap
70	Gas	80	Fuse

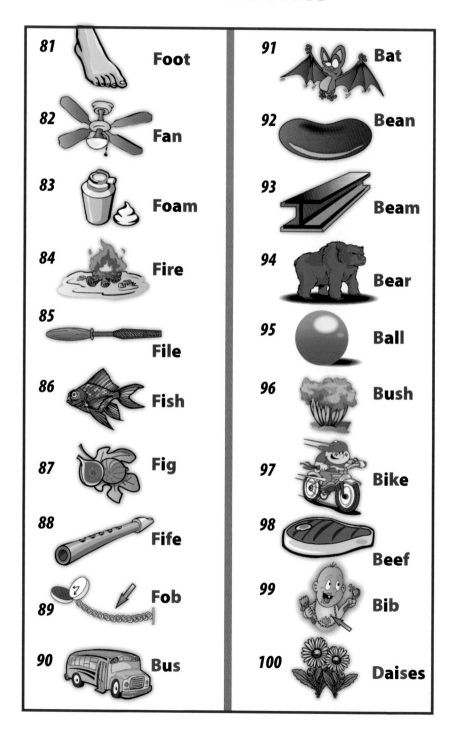

81 Foot

82 Fan

83 Foam

84 Fire

85 File

86 Fish

87 Fig

88 Fife

89 Fob

90 Bus

91 Bat

92 Bean

93 Beam

94 Bear

95 Ball

96 Bush

97 Bike

98 Beef

99 Bib

100 Daises

Remembering Dates

What can the list of words and numbers be used for? Numbers can be translated into words, and words can be *visualized* and *associated* with items, people, and events. So, an abstract number like 1903 (the year of the first flight by the Wright Brothers) becomes two words: Tub (T is 1, u has no numerical value, and b is 9) is the number 19. Mow (M has a numerical value of 3, and o and w have no numerical values) is the number 3. From this you get the Wright Brothers delivering by airplane a **tub** filled with a huge **mower** to celebrate their first flight.

The Scopes Trial took place in Dayton, Tennessee, in 1925. You already know that 19 is tub and 25 is nail, so you picture a giant nail piercing a tub that spills water on a ton of dates. Let's apply this technique to three other famous court cases:

Dred Scott v. Sandford (1857)

Buck v. Bell (1927)

Miranda v. Arizona (1966)

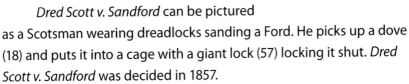

Let's apply this method to *Buck v. Bell.* The case can be visualized as a dollar bill (a buck) passing through the crack of the Liberty Bell. The year 1927 is a tub (19) with a nuke (27) resting inside. This dual image sits on top of the Liberty Bell with a buck inserted into its famous crack. *Buck v. Bell* was decided in 1927.

Dred Scott v. Sandford can be pictured as a Scotsman wearing dreadlocks sanding a Ford. He picks up a dove (18) and puts it into a cage with a giant lock (57) locking it shut. *Dred Scott v. Sandford* was decided in 1857.

Miranda v. Arizona (1966) could be recalled with an image of a young girl named Miranda holding a mirror in her hand as she rides to Arizona. The bus is pulling a tub (19) with a judge (66) sitting in it.

Miranda v. Arizona was decided in 1966. If all the court cases are in the 20th century, you won't need to use the tub image.

This system is not unique to me. I first saw it developed by David Roth in his book *The Famous Roth Memory Course*.[12] An early version was developed by Stanislaus Mink von Wennsshein around the year 1648. It was then modified extensively by a number of researchers in the memory development field. In 1808, Gregor von Feinaigle improved on the system by representing the numbers with consonant sounds. Roth's course, first published in 1918, is the most complete version of the method. Every book on memory published today follows the Roth method in some way.

So how is my approach different? I have tried to simplify the words used to represent numbers so the first letter sound identifies the numerical value. Notice how only two of Roth's first ten words (**c**ow and **sh**oe) begin with the actual letter sound representing 6 and 7:

Roth's First 10 Words

1. Hat
2. Hen
3. Ham
4. Hare
5. Hill
6. Shoe
7. Cow
8. Hive
9. Ape
10. Woods

While it will take some time to get comfortable with this memory technique, it will pay off with big dividends.

Learning a Piece of Pi

Once you master the 100-word system, you can amaze your friends by learning the value of Pi (π) to the 19th place (3.1415926535897932384) by converting words (letter sounds) into numbers:

> Madrid, Albany, Chile email a phobic bohemian mover

Ludolph van Ceulen (1540–1610) was the first to calculate pi to 35 digits. He was so pleased that he had them engraved on his tombstone.

By adding additional words and linking them to the above phrase, you can extend Pi to the 40th place (3.1415926535897932384 **62643383279502884197 1**):

China-jar-mom-famine-gap-lice-navy-ferret-bucket

Associate each word with the next word until you have them linked in order. Notice how some of the phrases tell a silly story. Practice writing the corresponding numbers without writing down the letters. Visualize the words and then convert the letter sounds into numbers. You can continue extending the place digits by adding more of your own words that correspond to the numbers. See how far you can get:

3.1415926535897932384626433832795028841971693993751058
2097494459230781640628620899862803482534211706798214
8086513282306647093844609550582231725359408128481174
5028410270193852110555964462294895493038196442881097
566593344612847564823378678316527120190914564 85.

There's a nifty program that will convert numbers into words based on the system presented in this chapter of *Memory Mechanics*. Type in a two to four digit number, and it will list numerous word options. You can download the program by going to http://got2know.net/2Know/.

> "The artificial memory is a memory strengthened or confirmed by training."
> —*Frances A. Yates*

In March 2004, Daniel Tammet from Kent, England, set a new European record when he recited from memory to 22,511 decimal places. It took him five hours to complete the task. Still, he had not broken the world record of 42,195 digits by Hiroyuki Goto of Japan set in 1995. The last time I checked, the record is now 67,890 by Lu Chao of China set in 2005.[13]

5

Help with Foreign Languages

Learning a language that does not use the English alphabet can present a challenge; this is especially true for a language like Hebrew. In addition to an unfamiliar alphabet, words are read from right to left. There are no vowel letters, but there are vowel pointings (dots and dashes) that identify vowel sounds. They appear as dots and dashes above and below the consonants, although you generally won't find them used in modern Hebrew writing (newspapers, signs, and novels), they are used in most biblical texts, prayer books, and books written for children. Even though the vowel pointings are not often used in modern Hebrew, the sounds are still there.

The first place to start in being able to read the Hebrew Bible is to become familiar with the Hebrew alphabet, then to build vocabulary. The more words you know, the easier it is to read any language. Language specialists recommend first learning words that appear most frequently. This can be difficult with some foreign languages since there are few English equivalents as compared to languages like Greek, Latin, Spanish, French, and Italian since the alphabet in most cases is similar to English. With a little creativity, this obstacle can be overcome by creating English words that mimic the sounds of the Hebrew words you are trying to learn. This can be done by developing a story sentence to help the memory process. (The best way to learn to speak a language is to hear it spoken and practice speaking. This is the way you learned English as a child. This is the way any language is learned well. Here we're dealing mainly with reading.)

In the first example below, the Hebrew word עם, reading right to left, is pronounced *ahm* which sounds something like "I'm." The English translation of *ahm* (עם) is **people**. You will need to use your imagination with this technique.

עם	*Ahm* speaking for the **people**. (I'm)
זקן	The **old man** has to use *zah geyn*. (the cane)
לקח	*Lah qakh* roach **takes** the crumbs I drop. (the cock roach)
ברית	*Bu reet* of his authority, the King made a **covenant** with his subjects. (By right)
כף	When I *kahph* I cover my mouth with my **hand**. (cough)
נשא	*Nasa* works **to lift up** great space ships. (NASA)
רוע	You will *rooah* the day you **shout** in this house. (rue)
קול	The *kohl* dust has affected my **voice**. (coal)
אדיר	*Ah deer* is a **mighty** runner. (A deer)
חזק	The Russian *Khazahq* has to be **strong**. (Cossack)
ילד	*Yah lahd* praised the mother who **bore** him. (The lad)
שוב	If you *shoov*, you can't **return** to the line. (shove)
בית	If you see a **house** you like, you should *bai yet*. (buy it)
עד	I thought he was *ahd* **until** I got to know him better. (odd)
כפר	The *kah phahr* will not **cover** the bed. (cover)
מנחה	*Min chan* not be saved by giving a **gift** to God. (Men can)
פתח	*Pa tahch* the key, and we can't **open** the door. (Pa took)
מן	Some *min* seem like they are **from** Mars. (men)

Most of these examples are from the Hebrew classes I took while a student at Reformed Theological Seminary. They were developed by Jack B. Scott. This technique can be applied to any foreign language.

6

Memory Feats

The opening scene of Alfred Hitchcock's *The 39 Steps* (1935) begins with "Mr. Memory" giving a demonstration of his impressive ability to answer any question asked of him by members of the audience. Mr. Memory is being used by spies to smuggle secrets out of England. He has them memorized. There is no paper trail since all the information is in Mr. Memory's head. The Air Ministry secrets were borrowed, memorized, and then replaced before anyone knew they had been missing

We are all impressed with people who sport a prodigious memory. There are even an infrequent number of savants who can remember seemingly endless lists of names and numbers. Who will ever forget Dustin Hoffman's portrayal of Raymond Babbit in the Academy Award-winning *Rain Man* (1988) and the restaurant scene with the telephone book and toothpicks? Given enough time, he would have memorized the entire telephone book.

Kim Peek, sometimes described as the "living Google," was the inspiration for the Raymond character. According to Peek's father, Kim was able to perform memory feats from the time he was 16-months old. He would read a book, remember nearly everything, and then place it upside down on the shelf to show that he had finished it. He reads a book in about an hour and remembers approximately 98% of everything he has read on every topic imaginable, from history, literature, and music to geography, sports, and the dates of common and obscure events and people. Give him your birth date, and he can tell you what day of the week it was. He has stored the information of more than 12,000 books in his memory.

Then there is Leslie Lemke who after hearing a song just once could play it on a piano without missing a note. Leslie never had a piano lesson.[14] In fact, he was blind and mentally disabled. His memory was extraordinary only in this one area. Beyond this unique ability, however, Leslie is completely dependent on the care of loving family members. This single gift of musical memory did not equip him to live beyond the confines of his sheltered existence.

Call out any date, and there are a rare number of people who can tell you the day of the week on which the date falls. No calculator is needed. No pencil or paper is required. In a matter of seconds the answer is given.

Richard Wawro visits a marketplace in Poland and several years later paints from memory a picture of it—in exquisite and minute detail. Ellen listens to an entire opera once or twice and then sings it back without error. George remembers what the weather was on every day of his adult life.[15]

There can be a downside to having a remarkable memory. Jill Price can recall in vivid detail every day of her life since age 14. She tells her story in *The Woman Who Can't Forget* (2008). Sounds like a great gift until you realize that a constant stream of decades of memories can overwhelm what needs to be known in the present. There is another downside to having a day-to-day autobiographical memory. Sometimes it's a blessing to forget.

Notes

1. David M. Roth, *Roth Memory Course* (New York: The Sun Dial Press, 1918), 1.

2. Joan Minninger, *Total Recall: How to Boost Your Memory Power* (Emmaus, PA: Rodale Press, 1984), 2.

3. Minninger, *Total Recall*, 2.

4. "Memory," *Newsweek* (September 29, 1986), 48.

5. "Memory," *Newsweek*, 48.

6. Julie Steenhuysen, "Bad grades? Faulty memory could be to blame" (March 2, 2008): http://www.reuters.com/article/scienceNews/idUSN02197961200 80302?feedType=RSS&feedName=scienceNews&rpc=22&sp=true

7. Sue Halpern, "Forgetting is the New Normal," *Time* (May 19, 2008), 43.

8. http://www.biblicalhebrew.com/alphabet.htm

9. This material is taken and adapted from Mary Carruthers and Jan M. Ziolkowski, eds., *The Medieval Craft of Memory: An Anthology of Texts and Pictures* (Philadelphia: University of Pennsylvania Press, 2002), 270–271.

10. Roth, *Roth Memory Course*, 2.

11. Joshua Foer, "Forget Me Not: How to Win the U.S. Memory Championship" (March 16, 2005): http://www.slate.com/id/2114925/fr/rss/

12. http://www.lybrary.com/roth-memory-course-p-57.html and http://books.google.com/books?id=6GON3Lr15vQC&pg=PA144&lpg=PA144&dq=roth+famous+memory+course&source=web&ots=uc8gwEoJOW&sig=BGmRJwjWaugy0j82dA87CwNRcdk&hl=en

13. http://pi-world-ranking-list.com/lists/memo/index.html

14. Shirlee Monty, *May's Boy: An Incredible Story of Love* (Nashville, TN: Thomas Nelson, 1981). In 1983, ABC aired a drama about Leslie and his adoptive mother, called *The Woman Who Willed a Miracle*, starring Cloris Leachman as May, Leslie's adoptive mother. See the following for more information: http://www.wisconsinmedicalsociety.org/savant_syndrome/savant_profiles/leslie_lemke

15. Darold A. Treffert, *Extraordinary People: Understanding "Idiot Savants"* (New York: Harper & Row, 1989), 165.

Visit
www.MemoryMechanics.com
for additional techniques and valuable information
to improve your memory.

AMERICAN VISION
A Biblical Worldview Ministry

P.O. Box 220
Powder Springs, GA 40127

www.AmericanVision.org
1.800.628.9460